Imagine
Create
Draw
Write

BLUEFIELDS™

Welcome to Bluefields friends. Are you ready to learn how to count to ten? Let's turn the page and begin!

How many frogs
do you see?

Let's count.

How many pumpkins
do you see?

Let's count.

How many candy
corns do you see?

Let's count.

How many spiders
do you see?

Let's count.

How many cats
do you see?

Let's count.

How many flying
bugs do you see?

Let's count.

How many ghosts do you see?

Let's count.

How many owls
do you see?

Let's count.

How many UFO's
do you see?

Let's count.

How many bats
do you see?

Let's count.

I hope you enjoyed learning to count to ten
with the Bluefields' friends.

Why not go back to the beginning of the book
and count again?

*This book and other great titles by Captain Spooky Cooky
are available for sale on Amazon.*